Happy Birthday
Brenda

I love my very
very special
friend,

Barbara

Happy Birthday to you

pictures and verse
by
Sandra Magsamen

gift

stewart tabori & chang

You have never looked better,

your
smile
is
so
bright...

you are as brillant as a big vibrant light.

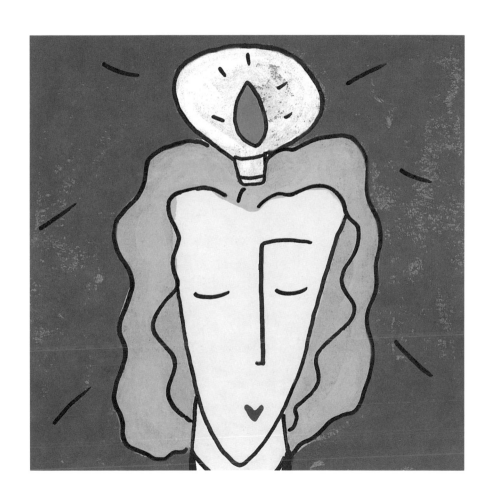

Your spirit
is kind,
compassionate
and giving
too.

and you still joyfully dance in your "birthday suit" when the spirit moves you.

Your laughter
sparkles and
glows like
the candles
on your cake...

and your
loyalty, honesty
and caring
account for the
friends that
you make.

You are
playful,
humorous
and a lot
of fun too...

By listening to yourself, You have learned to trust in all that you do.

Your great
big heart
gives everyone
around you
a lift.

You
are a
beautiful
gift.

You believe that wishes do come true.

There is a little piece of magic in all that you do.

You've got attitude, style and grace...

Happy
Birthday
to a wonderful
member of the
human race.

Pictures and verse by Sandra Magsamen
© 2000 Hanny Girl Productions, Inc.
Exclusive licensing agent Momentum Partners, Inc., NY, NY

Published in 2000 by
Stewart, Tabori & Chang
A division of U.S. Media Holdings, Inc.
115 West 18th Street
New York, NY 10011

Distributed in Canada by
General Publishing Company Ltd.
30 Lesmill Road
Don Mills, Ontario, Canada M3B 2T6

ISBN: 1-58479-005-9

Printed in Hong Kong

10 9 8 7 6 5 4 3 2 1